SIGHTSEERS
ESSENTIAL TRAVEL GUIDES TO THE PAST

ANCIENT ROME

A GUIDE TO THE GLORY
OF IMPERIAL ROME

JONATHAN STROUD

KINGfISHER

KINGFISHER
Kingfisher Publications Plc
New Penderel House,
283–288 High Holborn,
London WC1V 7HZ
www.kingfisherpub.com

Written and edited by   Jonathan Stroud
Designer   Malcolm Parchment

Consultant   David Nightingale
Illustrations   Inklink Firenze
Kevin Maddison

DTP Co-ordinator   Nicky Studdart
Production Controllers   Kelly Johnson
Jacquie Horner
Picture Research Manager   Jane Lambert
Proofreader   Emma Wild
Indexer   Sylvia Potter

First published by Kingfisher Publications Plc 2000
3 5 7 9 10 8 6 4 2

2TR/0501/WKT/AT(AT)/140MA

A CIP catalogue record for this book is available from
the British Library.

ISBN 0 7534 0411 7

Printed in
Hong Kong/China

Contents

Introducing Rome

Welcome to Rome, greatest city in the world. It is the heart of the largest empire ever seen, ruling over millions of people from places as far apart as Britain and Egypt. Above all it is a city of extremes. Filled with spacious palaces and public buildings, it is also the most crowded site on Earth. One million people live here, crammed into the narrow streets. And although the Empire's riches pour into Rome, over 200,000 people are out of work and rely on the emperor for free grain.

The emperor Hadrian is rarely in Rome itself. He spends years travelling through the Empire, protecting its frontiers and exploring many local cultures. However, he has still found time to organize new building projects in his capital.

According to legend, Rome was founded by Romulus. He and his brother were abandoned here as babies, and cared for by a wolf.

For centuries, Rome was ruled by a senate of important men. SPQR stands for *"the Senate and the People of Rome"*.

Rome's first rival was the African city of Carthage. Its army used elephants to attack Italy, but they were defeated.

Rome's weather is good, and people spend most of the time outdoors.

In the Forum, look for the Rostra platform where political speeches are made.

Rome has grown beyond its walls. Its empire is so strong, it needs no defence.

Rome's spiritual heart is the ancient Roman Forum, or market place. Centuries ago, when Rome was a village, its people met in this open space to trade and discuss politics. Now the old square is built up with giant temples and political memorials, and the markets have moved elsewhere. The old ruling Senate House is still by the Forum, but Rome's real centre of power is now the emperor's palace nearby.

Sightseers' tip

You will see vast differences in wealth here in Rome. A tiny elite is staggeringly rich, but one third of its people are slaves.

For 250 years after beating Carthage, Rome's efficient armies conquered all the lands round the Mediterranean Sea.

A great general, Julius Caesar, destroyed the Senate's power and ruled Rome alone, but he was murdered by the senators.

After Caesar's death, his adopted son Augustus took control. He became the first in a long line of emperors.

5

Travelling around

Y ou'll have no problem getting to Rome. It is the centre of the finest road system ever constructed. There are over 50,000 kilometres of superb highway covering the Empire, all built by the Roman army. Communications are easier now than at any time in history, and you could cross the Empire in just 100 days on horseback. Once you're in Rome itself, however, it's not always easy finding your way about. None of the thousands of winding streets have names or numbers.

If you can hitch a lift on a merchant ship, a great way to get to Rome is up the River Tiber. Hundreds of small craft sail to and from the coast, bringing grain, wine and other supplies that the city needs.

A new road is given very hard-wearing foundations. A flat layer of sand goes on the bottom, with layers of stone and gravel above. The road is topped with paving stones, which are humped to let rain run off. Road engineers use tools to keep their course as straight as possible, so that all distances are minimized.

On the way to Rome, look out for milestones that tell you how far you've got to go.

If you get lost in the city, use temples and statues as landmarks to find your way.

Take a slave with you if you go out at night. Thieves and muggers are common in Rome.

Sightseers' tip If you're caught short in the street, look for a urine jar. The contents of these are sold to cloth makers, who use it to dissolve fat and grease left in fresh wool.

Although rich people might travel about by sedan chair, by far the best way to get around Rome is on foot. There are raised pavements to keep you out of the mud and sewage on the roads, and stepping stones to help you cross. Walking also keeps you mobile in the main streets, which stay busy even at night. Traders with noisy, slow-moving carts are only allowed into the city at dusk, and soon block the streets. Traffic jams are common, and so are lost tempers.

What to wear

Romans pay a lot of attention to their appearance, and you should fit in with their current styles. For instance, men have traditionally been clean-shaven, but the emperor has just begun a new fashion for wearing beards. Old-style togas are still worn for important occasions, but for day-to-day use, the simpler tunic is now preferred.

Rich women have personal slaves to shape their hair in elaborate styles. This can take all morning. Others wear wigs made from the hair of foreign slaves – blonde hair from German women is thought to be very exotic.

Romans have plenty of tools to help improve their looks. You can invest in combs, hairpins, tweezers for plucking hairs, and special small spoons for scooping wax out of your ears.

You can buy stick-on leather patches to cover any nasty spots or scars.

Men must wear their togas when visiting the law courts or on official business.

Roman women often use crushed ants' egg paste to darken their eyebrows.

Both men and women wear jewellery, including brooches to hold their cloaks in place. Snake bracelets are popular, and so are gold necklaces set with precious stones.

Sightseers' tip

For women, a pale face is a sign of status. Poor women have rough, red faces from working in the open. Use creams of chalk, flour and lead to whiten your skin.

A fashionable Roman woman takes great care with her clothes. She first puts on an ankle-length woollen under-tunic, with a colourful embroidered dress, or *stola*, on top. This can be made of wool, cotton or silk. She then places a beautiful jewelled girdle around her waist. Wealthy men wear long tunics. Poorer men and slaves have shorter tunics, which give their legs more freedom as they work.

Food and drink

What you eat in Rome will depend on one simple thing: money. If you're rich, you'll taste an unending array of exotic delicacies – from stuffed dormice to ostrich and flamingo. If not, you'll share most people's diet of grain boiled into porridge and mixed with cheap foods like eggs and cheese. For these Romans, meat is a rare dish. Whoever you are, wine mixed with water is the usual drink. It is considered vulgar to drink wine undiluted.

Roman kitchens contain many spices and herbs. Spicy sauces are put on everything to cover the rotting taste of old meat or fish. The favourite sauce is *liquamen*, strained from salted fish guts left out in the sun.

Ovens are banned in Rome's crowded flats, because of the risk of fire. So many people don't cook at all, but visit streetside taverns to buy good food such as soup, sausages, pies, fried fish and fruit. Other favourites include thin round pastries topped with olives, fish and onions. Tasty snacks like this are perfect for a midday meal.

At some parties, dancing and music is laid on while guests eat.

Rome is a day's journey from the sea, so fish here is seldom fresh!

Need a cure for indigestion? Try raw cabbage soaked in vinegar.

Hosts holding parties seek to impress their guests with the very finest silver dishes. Salads and oysters are often brought out for starters, followed by several courses of game birds, boar, venison, hare, ham and fish. Meals end with honey cakes and fruit.

Sightseers' tip

At some big banquets with huge amounts of food, a room is set aside as a *vomitorium* for those who eat too much too soon. By making yourself sick there, you can empty your stomach ready for the next few courses!

At most dinner parties, the guests recline on three couches around a table. They support themselves on the left elbow, and hold their food in the right hand. Knives or spoons are rarely used, so most foods are quite solid and not served too hot. The host's slaves serve everyone, but guests sometimes bring their own slaves along to help out.

Shopping

Rome is the most incredible shopping centre on Earth. Every day, ships and wagons arrive from all over the Empire, carrying goods made in distant corners of the world. Traders from as far as India and China bring back luxury silks and spices to delight the wealthy buyers here. But there are countless affordable things to buy too: whether you're after shoes, pots or clothes, you'll find exactly what you want in Rome.

Rome is the richest city in the Empire, and luxury goods are plentiful here. This vase, specially carved out of blue and white glass, would have taken months to make, and can be afforded only by the super-rich.

Most Roman shops are stalls or rooms opening out on to the street. Here you can buy many exotic things: wool from Britain, silver from Spain, carpets from Turkey and perfumes from Iran. But of all the goods on sale, by far the most important are the huge amounts of grain that arrive daily from Africa. Rome is so big that Italian farmers can't supply enough wheat, so imports are essential if the poor are to be kept alive. In hard times, the emperor gives free hand-outs of grain to the needy.

The newest and most spectacular place to browse in Rome is Trajan's Market near the Forum. Made using the latest technology, it is a massive semi-circular shopping centre carved out of the side of a hill, with 150 shops, offices and a central open space where traders can set up their stalls.

To find a tavern, look for green boughs hanging over the door.

The same coinage is used across the Empire, from Asia Minor to Britain.

The best mass-produced red pottery comes from France.

Sightseers' tip

If you're a woman, don't be seen shopping for anything other than perfume, jewellery or clothes. Most ordinary shopping is done by male slaves.

Slaves are brought to Rome from battlefields at the edges of the Empire. You can pick them for their strength or looks, or for skills such as dancing, cookery or music. Talented slaves can cost 12 times as much as unskilled ones.

Accommodation

There are great differences in the quality of housing in Rome. The city sprawls over seven hills and all the richest people live in spacious villas on the airy higher ground. Everyone else is crammed into ramshackle blocks of flats filling the valleys in between. In summer, these hot, over-crowded streets are a breeding-ground for disease, and the few who can afford it leave the city for the country. Rich or poor, most people don't spend much time at home – they prefer to work and socialize outdoors, or in public places, such as the baths.

Sightseers' tip

Look out for the *vigiles*, Rome's seven squads of professional firemen. Each squad has 1,000 freedmen who tackle fires, and help keep order on the rowdy streets.

Unless you're very rich, you'll have to find lodging in one of the crowded tenement buildings that house most of Rome's people. It is a risky business – the stuffy flats are vulnerable to fire, and are so poorly made that they often fall down. Each block has up to six storeys, with shops on the ground floor. Try for a room at the top – or the noise of traders' carts will keep you awake all night!

People with rooms to let often paint 'For Rent' on the side of the building.

Most houses are airy to keep you cool in summer. In winter, they can be freezing!

The father is head of the family, but his wife runs all household affairs.

A rich man's town house is centred upon the *atrium*, an open hall with a pool in the centre to catch water. Doors to the dining room, reception rooms, kitchen and bedrooms lead off on either side. The *atrium* is the house's main source of light and air – outside walls have few windows, to keep out noise and burglars. At the back, a *peristyle*, or garden, filled with shrubs and statues, provides a tranquil spot for the family to escape the city's hubbub.

Even big houses don't have much furniture. The couches in the dining room are the most important items. By adding a woollen blanket, they double up as beds at night.

Many houses have small shrines where families worship their own personal gods, called *lares*. Every day, offerings of wine, cakes and incense are made at the shrines, which contain tiny statues of the *lar*. If the offerings are given correctly, the *lar* will bring wealth and happiness to his household.

The baths

The public baths are an essential part of life in Rome. There are hundreds of baths in the city, and many people visit one every day to spend a few relaxing hours swimming, chatting or playing games in magnificent surroundings. Most trips to the baths are free, because rich men pay everyone's fees in the hope of gaining votes or increasing their popularity.

For the Romans, personal hygiene is vital. Clean yourself by rubbing oil into your skin, then scraping off the mingled oil and dirt with a blunt metal tool called a *strigil*.

Sightseers' tip

Watch out! Water in steam baths is heated by air from underground furnaces, so the floor tiles are scalding. You may wish to wear sandals to protect your feet.

Hire a slave to guard your clothes – or they might be stolen.

Men and women bathe separately. A bell signals the change-over.

Slaves sell tasty snacks to help you recover after a long swim.

All the baths are very richly decorated. There are intricate mosaics on the floor, rooms are lined with marble pillars, and the ceilings are high and beautifully painted. All this luxury gives even poor people a regular taste of the power and wealth of Rome.

Look out for the splendid public lavatories at the baths. Some can sit 16 people side by side, so you can chat to your friends with ease. This is better than toilets at home, which are often simply pots in the corner.

There are a bewildering variety of rooms in the baths. They include hot and cold pools, steam rooms, saunas and haircutting salons. The largest baths also have forecourts with shops, restaurants and libraries. When you visit, warm up in the gymnasium by wrestling or playing ball games, then make for the *caldarium* – the hottest room of all – to bring yourself out in a cleansing sweat. After a good massage, finish with an invigorating dip in the ice-cold plunge pool.

The theatre

Visiting the theatre is one of the Romans' favourite pastimes. There are several semi-circular stone theatres in the city, hosting plays and games to celebrate recent victories. Shows last many hours, and there are several kinds to see. Although some Greek tragedies are shown, Romans are more keen on comedy, with lots of crude jokes, fast action and happy endings. Some characters are very popular, such as the cunning slave, who always manages to talk himself out of trouble in the nick of time.

Sightseers' tip

Don't hire rooms near a theatre. To get good seats, a crowd will gather the night before a show – and they make a lot of noise. The emperor Caligula once ordered his guards to beat up a crowd after they kept him awake all night!

Free food and drink is usually provided by the show's sponsor.

Theatres sometimes bring wild beasts on stage to attract larger crowds.

For some tragedies, a real-life criminal might be executed live on stage.

Actors rehearse in the building behind the back of the stage. They are all men, but they play many women's roles too.

Romans love special effects – ghosts appear through holes in the stage floor and winches help produce gods from above. There is little scenery, although real chariots and horses can appear on stage. Actors wear standardized masks, wigs and colours to show what kind of character they are playing. If the crowd is pleased, they clap, snap their fingers and thumbs and wave their togas – but if not, they will hiss, shout and make rude noises.

Music and songs accompany many plays. Greek instruments such as the stringed lyre or *cithara* are popular, and so are the double pipes, cymbals and tamborine, which can all be heard well in the open air.

The temples

Religion is an important part of life in Rome. Everything from personal health to success in war depends on the favour of the gods, and regular rituals must be carried out to keep them satisfied. In hundreds of temples across the city, special priests elected from among Rome's nobles perform sacrifices on behalf of the people. Festivals and feast days are held for each god, and offerings of fruit, wine and animals are made each day.

Jupiter is the king of the gods, and Rome itself is under his protection. He also controls the sky and weather. Many other gods watch over every aspect of life. Some of the most important are Mars, the god of war, Apollo, the god of light and music, Vesta, the goddess of home and hearth, and Minerva, the goddess of wisdom.

Sightseers' tip Want to know your destiny? The Romans are keen on divination – the interpretation of omens. Thunder, lightning and the behaviour of birds are studied and used to predict the future.

Sacred chickens are watched for omens during army campaigns.

During *Saturnalia*, the winter festival, people give each other presents.

Hadrian is said to have designed the Pantheon's dome himself.

Animal sacrifices are often carried out. Each animal must be a perfect physical specimen, and the more willingly it goes to the slaughter, the better the omen. Once dead, its entrails are studied: if they are in good condition, the body is cooked for the pleasure of the gods.

If you are ill and need a god's help, your prayers must be accompanied by a gift. Leave a model of the sick part of your body at the temple.

The newest and one of the greatest sights in Rome is Hadrian's Pantheon, a temple to all the gods. It is a masterpiece of engineering, with the world's widest dome (43m), made from concrete poured over a temporary wooden framework. Statues of the gods line the walls. A single hole at the top, the *oculus*, provides the only light and represents the sun in the heavens.

Circus Maximus

If there's one unmissable sight in Rome, it's the Circus Maximus. This giant chariot-racing circuit is over 500 years old, and is by far the biggest stadium in the world. Up to 250,000 people can crowd in to watch the races – that's a quarter of Rome's population! Everyone comes here to cheer on their teams and gasp at the high-speed crashes. Entry is free to watch all the day's 24 races.

If you enjoy a flutter – beware! You can bet on chariot races and gladiator fights, but it is illegal at other times. Still, Romans love gambling, and many go to secret betting houses, where they can wager money on dice or on the tossing of coins.

Sightseers' tip
Keep an eye out for cheating. Drivers have been known to slip a stick through their rivals' spokes to make them crash.

Races start when an official drops a handkerchief. There are four teams in each race, the blues, whites, reds and greens. Each race lasts for seven 1.5km laps of the wall or *spina* at the centre of the arena.

The Circus is a very popular place for secret meetings between lovers.

Track marshals stand by to throw water on the smouldering wheels of crashed chariots.

 Look out for seven dolphins on the *spina*. One is removed to mark each lap.

Chariot racing is popular with all age groups. Children from wealthy families are given small chariots to play in, pulled by donkeys or even goats!

Each chariot is as light and mobile as possible, but they are very flimsy and can easily overturn. The most dangerous parts of the course are the corners. It is very difficult to turn the chariots at high speeds and collisions are common. Drivers try to drive their opponents into the wall. Each driver has only leather thongs to protect his body, and if he does have a "shipwreck" he is likely to be badly injured or killed.

23

The Colosseum

No visitor to Rome should miss the impressive Flavian Amphitheatre – also known as the Colosseum – which can be seen from all over the city. It is the biggest amphitheatre in the world, and can hold a staggering 55,000 spectators. Try to visit on a public holiday, when everyone can get in free to watch the spectacular and bloodthirsty shows that take place there.

Exotic creatures from all over the known world are brought to Rome to appear at the Colosseum. The crowd's favourites are the ferocious lions, which are set loose to devour helpless criminals.

Gladiators are either slaves, prisoners or criminals. If they entertain the crowd they may get gifts of coins, but only those who survive many fights will be set free. These lucky few are given bone tablets with their names on to prove they are now free men.

Don't worry about the huge crowds at the Colosseum – there are 80 entrances, so you'll be able to find a seat quickly. When you are inside, your head will be protected from the strong sun by an enormous canvas awning that can be moved back and forth by teams of slaves pulling on hundreds of ropes outside.

24

To keep the people happy, there are over 100 public holidays in Rome every year.

 Prisoners and wild beasts are kept in a maze of cages under the arena's floor.

Why not place a bet on your favourite gladiator? If he wins his fight, you'll be rich!

Gladiators are the most popular entertainment here. Many fighters come out onto the arena together, and lots are drawn to see which men will fight each other to the death. There are several different types of gladiator, each with their own weapons, armour, strengths and weaknesses.

Many spectators love the brave and nimble *retarius*, who tries to snare his enemy in a net and then stab him with his trident. Others prefer the *secutor*, whose weighty equipment makes him slow but powerful.

Heavy helmets give gladiators protection, but they are difficult to see out of, which is risky when fighting a fast opponent.

Sightseers' tip Watch for the emperor, as he decides whether a beaten gladiator should live or die. If he gives the thumbs up, the man will live – but if it is thumbs down, he will be killed by his opponent.

Around Rome

Although the city of Rome dominates this part of Italy, it is well worth taking a trip to the beautiful countryside beyond it. The way of life is slower here, but it is crucial to the well-being of the Empire. Much of the land is covered by vast farm estates, owned by the wealthiest men in Rome, which supply much of the food that keeps the city going. Wine and olive oil are the most important crops. They are carried in huge quantities to giant ports on the Mediterranean coast and exported by sea all over the Empire.

Sightseers' tip Try and buy fresh honey made in one of the estates' beehives. It is the only way to sweeten your food.

Just 25km from Rome at the mouth of the River Tiber, Ostia is the world's busiest port. The emperors have widened its harbour several times to cope with the huge numbers of ships. Massive warehouses on the seafront store grain, wine and olive oil before barges take them up the Tiber to Rome.

Poor quality grapes are made into wine for workers to drink.

Farms are run by the manager, the *vilicus*. He is often a trusted slave.

Although the mild climate is good for crops, the Italian soil is often poor.

Most rich families only visit the estates in the summer to get out of the sweltering city. But there is a workforce of slaves on the farms year-round to tend to the crops and livestock.

A nobleman's villa sits at the heart of each estate, surrounded by houses for slaves and farm workers, market gardens and vineyards. In the autumn, the grapes are picked and crushed by slaves to extract the juice. This is poured into large half-buried jars to ferment and become wine. The jars are sealed with pitch to keep out the rain.

When the olives are harvested from the trees, they are piled into an olive press. Slaves pull the handles down to squash the olives and squeeze the oil out into a jar.

All around Rome, gigantic aqueducts radiate out across the countryside to distant water sources. They supply over 40 million gallons of water to the city every day, mostly to baths and fountains. The water moves by gravity, so each aqueduct must constantly angle downhill along all its length. At the top, stone slabs cover the water channel to keep out dirt.

Survival guide

Rome is a vibrant, cosmopolitan city filled with visitors from lands all over the Empire. It has everything you need to enjoy your stay. However, it is also a place where laws are strictly enforced, and it is vital that you do not fall foul of the authorities, who will punish non-citizens severely for any misdemeanour.

Magistrates are still officially elected to public posts by Rome's citizens. To win support, these rich men will spend massive sums on pleasing the people.

Society

Visitors must be aware of the rigidly defined levels of Roman society. At the top are Roman citizens, who are divided into the wealthy nobility and the ordinary people, or *plebeians*. Non-citizens from outside Rome have fewer rights. Below all these are the slaves, who do most of the work in farm and city. Slaves have almost no rights at all, but they can be freed if their master chooses. Hadrian has just passed a law forbidding masters from killing slaves without a trial.

Administration

The emperor has absolute power. He appoints all the most important officials, who come from the rich nobility. Wealthy young men follow political careers, as lawyers, magistrates, and finally as the governors of far-flung regions of the Empire.

Surgeons have sophisticated tools to operate on wounds and broken bones, but the only pain-killers available are poppy juice and wine.

Non-citizens and slaves who steal from a temple are thrown to wild animals.

To prevent uprisings, the Praetorian Guard is the only legion allowed near Rome.

Romans are tolerant of different religions, but Christians are sometimes persecuted.

Four squads of special legionaries carry out police duties in Rome. In times of serious disturbance, the Praetorian Guard are called in.

Law and Order

The Romans are very keen on discipline and you would be wise not to break their laws during your stay. Minor crimes are punished by beatings. Thieves are branded. For the worst offences, slaves can be executed by crucifixion. An elite force of legionaries, the Praetorian Guard, protects the body of the emperor himself.

Health

Medicine is based largely on herbal remedies and is not always very effective. For broken ribs, for example, the writer Pliny recommends applying a mix of goat's dung and wine to the wound.

Some slaves wear special tags with their master's name and address on. If they run away, they can be caught and returned.

29

? Souvenir quiz

By the time you leave Rome, you will have seen many amazing things. Before you go, find out how much you remember about your visit by trying this special souvenir quiz. Answers are on page 32.

1. The Roman Forum is the most historic site in the city. How did it first start out?

a) As a hilltop fortress.

b) As a market place in a village.

c) As a temple to Romulus, founder of Rome.

2. What kind of creature cared for Romulus as a baby?

a) A wolf.

b) A bear.

c) An eagle.

3. What will keep you awake if you hire a room near street level?

a) Traders' carts bringing goods into the city at night.

b) All-night chariot races through the streets.

c) Drunken revellers on their way home from wild parties.

4. What do fashionable Roman women make wigs out of?

a) Horse hair from Arabian stallions.

b) Human hair from slaves.

c) Finely spun silk from the Far East.

5. Why would a Roman woman want to have a pale face?

a) It proves she's of pure Roman blood.

b) It is considered to be a sign of great health.

c) It proves she is rich enough to stay indoors and not do any work.

6. Precious goods are brought to Rome from all over the known world. But what is Rome's most vital import?

a) Swords from Asia Minor.

b) Grain from Africa.

c) Tea cups from Britain.

7. What is *liquamen*?

a) A mix of rotting fish guts and salt used as a sauce.

b) A strong alcoholic drink made from cranberries.

c) A mix of boars' droppings and wine used to treat bad chest injuries.

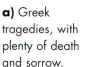

8. What equipment does the *retarius* gladiator carry?

a) A weighted net and a trident.

b) A short sword and a heavy rectangular shield.

c) A light javelin and a round shield.

9. The *lares* are very important to most Romans. But who are they?

a) Rome's special fire brigade.

b) The chief priests of Jupiter working at the Pantheon.

c) Household gods who watch over each family.

10. What are "shipwrecks" and where do people go to watch them?

a) Merchant ships running aground in the harbour at Ostia.

b) Rich men's sedan chairs colliding in the Roman Forum.

c) Chariots crashing at the Circus Maximus.

11. Romans love going to the theatre. What kind of play do they most like to see?

a) Greek tragedies, with plenty of death and sorrow.

b) Fast-paced comedies, with lots of farcical situations and silly jokes.

c) Political satires, filled with angry jokes at the emperor's expense.

Index

Acknowledgements

The consultant
David Nightingale M.A. (Oxon) teaches Greek and Roman history at the University of Kent at Canterbury. He is a regular visitor to Rome and Italy.

Inklink Firenze illustrators
Simone Boni, Alessandro Rabatti, Lorenzo Pieri, Luigi Critone, Lucia Mattioli, Francisco Petracchi, Theo Caneschi, Federico Ferniani, Alain Bressan, Concetta D'Amato.

Additional illustrations
Richard Berridge, Luigi Galante, Nicki Palin, Thomas Troyer.

Picture credits
b = bottom, c = centre, l = left, r = right, t = top
p.4cl The Bridgeman Art Library, London/New York/Museo
Archeologico Nazionale, Naples; p.6cl AKG London/Erich Lessing; p.9tr The British Museum; c Scala; p.11tr The Bridgeman Art Library, London/New York/Louvre, Paris, France; p.12c Ancient Art & Architecture; p.15br The British Museum; p.17tr Ancient Art & Architecture; p.19tl Ancient Art & Architecture; p.20bl C M Dixon/British Museum; p.23tl Giraudon/Louvre, Paris; p.25cr AKG London/Museum für Deutsche Geschichte, Berlin; p.27cr AKG London/Erich Lessing; p.28br Scala

Every effort has been made to trace the copyright holders of the photographs. The publishers apologise for any inconvenience caused.

This book is set in the year AD128.

Souvenir quiz answers

1 = b) 2 = a) 3 = a) 4 = b) 5 = c) 6 = b) 7 = a) 8 = a) 9 = c) 10 = c) 11 = b)